I0454353

THE DATA-MARKETING BIBLE

MAURICIO VELLASQUEZ

Copyright © 2023 Mauricio Vellasquez

CONTENT

1 DIGITAL MARKETING X DATA SCIENCE

Digital transformation is not a new phenomenon, but its impact continues to redefine various industries, with advertising being one of them. The advent of the internet brought along a new domain for advertisers to explore. The digital era not only broadened the reach of advertising, but also introduced a new dynamic in how advertising campaigns are conceived, executed, and evaluated.

At the heart of this digital revolution lies a commodity that has become as valuable as gold - data. In this digital landscape, every interaction, every click, every purchase leaves digital traces that, when aggregated and analyzed, unveil patterns and insights that were previously invisible to the eyes of advertisers.

Online advertising has grown exponentially since its infancy with the floating banners of the 90s. It has evolved into a robust ecosystem that includes search engine advertising, social media advertising, content marketing, email marketing, and much more. This diversity has allowed advertisers a deeper segmentation and the ability to reach their target audiences in more meaningful ways.

Data: The New Frontier

Data has been a catalytic force behind this evolution. It enables a deeper understanding of consumer behavior and preferences. With the aid of advanced analytical tools, advertisers can now create more personalized campaigns, measure ROI (Return on Investment) more accurately, and optimize their strategies in real time.

Data analysis not only provides advertisers with a clear view of campaign performance, but also unveils opportunities for enhanced engagement and conversion. It's now possible to better understand what resonates with the audience and dynamically adjust messages to cater to their preferences.

Online advertising campaigns, now armed with detailed data and precise insights, are achieving levels of efficiency and personalization that were unimaginable just a decade ago. Let's explore further how this is being accomplished.

Predictive Analysis

One of the most powerful applications of data science in advertising is predictive analysis. By analyzing vast sets of historical data, advertisers can predict future trends, consumer behaviors, and the potential success of advertising campaigns. This foresight allows for more effective resource allocation and more informed advertising strategies.

Audience Segmentation

Data science enables more precise audience segmentation. Previously, audience segments were quite generic and based on basic demographic information. Now, with advanced data analysis, advertisers can create much more specific audience segments based on a variety of criteria, including online behaviors, purchase history, preferences, and much more.

Real-Time Campaign Optimization

With data flowing in real time, advertisers now have the ability to optimize campaigns while they are being executed. This can include adjustments in advertising messages, budget reallocation to higher-performing channels, or modification of creatives to resonate better with the audience.

Programmatic Advertising

Programmatic advertising, which is the automated purchasing of advertising space using algorithms and data to make decisions in milliseconds, is another offspring of the data revolution. It allows ads to be more relevant to the audience and achieves operational efficiency by eliminating many of the manual tasks associated with media buying.

Performance Measurement and ROI

With data science, the measurement of campaign performance has become more accurate. Advertisers can track a variety of metrics to understand the ROI of their campaigns and make adjustments as necessary.

Actionable Insights

Lastly, and perhaps most importantly, data science provides actionable insights. Instead of guessing what may or may not work, advertisers can make decisions based on real data and insights, making campaigns more effective and efficient.

Now, we find ourselves on the brink of a new horizon

where data is redefining what is possible in the world of online advertising. They are not only improving the performance of existing campaigns, but also opening doors to innovations in how we interact with and understand our audience. With the rise of artificial intelligence and machine learning, online advertising is bound to become more effective, interactive, and personalized.

This is just the beginning of the journey. How will data continue to transform online advertising? In what ways can they be utilized to optimize online advertising campaigns? The answers to these questions promise to not only reshape the advertising industry but also redefine the relationship between brands and consumers in the digital era.

As we embark on this exploration, we will unravel how data science is creating a new paradigm in online advertising, providing an undeniable competitive advantage for those who know how to effectively harness the power of data.

2 FROM BITS TO BIG DATA

The digital universe is composed of an infinity of bits, the smallest units of data, represented by zeros and ones. These bits, when combined in complex sequences, form the foundation for all the digital information that circulates through cyberspace. However, it was the aggregation of these bits into massive volumes, known as Big Data, that triggered a revolution in the way information is processed, analyzed, and utilized, especially in the field of online advertising.

The journey of Big Data begins with the collection of these bits of information, which today occurs on an unprecedented scale. Every click on a website, every like on a social media post, every online purchase contributes to the growing ocean of data. This phenomenon is amplified by the proliferation of connected devices, from smartphones to connected cars and smart appliances, that are constantly generating and transmitting data.

Once collected, this data is stored in robust and flexible data storage infrastructures that can accommodate the exponential growth of data. Cloud computing platforms, such as AWS, Azure, and Google Cloud, have played a crucial role in providing the necessary storage and processing capacity to handle Big Data.

The subsequent step is the analysis of this data. Here, data science comes into play, employing a variety of techniques and tools to extract valuable insights from these vast data sets. Sophisticated algorithms, machine learning, and artificial intelligence are applied to identify patterns, predict trends, and inform business decisions.

In the realm of online advertising, Big Data is a gold mine of insights. It provides advertisers with a deeper and nuanced understanding of consumer behavior and preferences. For instance, data can reveal which types of ads resonate more with different audience segments, when and where these ads are most likely to be viewed and clicked, and how different advertising campaigns contribute to conversions and customer engagement.

Data is also fundamental for the effectiveness of programmatic advertising, which uses algorithms to automate the buying of ad space, ensuring that ads reach the right audience at the right time and in the right context. Real-time data analysis allows advertisers to adjust their campaigns on-the-fly to improve performance and ROI.

However, the Big Data revolution also brings challenges. Privacy and consent issues are at the center of the debate on how data should be collected, stored, and used. Moreover, the ability to analyze and correctly interpret data is a crucial skill set, but still lacking in many sectors of the industry.

Big Data is also driving continuous innovation in advertising technology. For instance, emerging technologies such as augmented reality (AR) and virtual reality (VR) are beginning to be explored to offer more immersive and engaging advertising experiences, fueled by insights derived from Big Data.

The journey of Big Data is undoubtedly a journey of continuous discovery and innovation. As we progress into the digital era, the central role of Big Data in defining the future of online advertising will continue to grow, opening new frontiers of possibilities in the connection between brands and consumers. From the need to handle a large amount of data with consequent great complexity, data science emerges.

Data science emerged as an interdisciplinary field dedicated to extracting knowledge and insights from data. Combining statistics, machine learning, predictive analysis, and other analytical techniques, data science has provided a deeper understanding of the phenomena represented by the data.

The exponential growth of data science can be attributed to several factors:

Technological Advances: The evolution of data storage and processing technologies, including cloud computing and distributed processing frameworks like Hadoop and Spark, have facilitated the handling of large data sets. These technologies not only provided the ability to store and process Big Data, but also accelerated the speed at which data can be analyzed, allowing for real-time or near real-time insights.

Data Accessibility: The proliferation of internet-connected devices, including smartphones and other IoT (Internet of Things) devices, resulted in an explosion of data available for analysis. Every connected device is a potential source of data, providing a continuous stream of information that can be utilized to enhance products, services, and marketing strategies.

Algorithm Development: The continuous development of advanced algorithms and machine learning and deep learning techniques has allowed for data to be analyzed in more sophisticated ways. More advanced algorithms can identify complex and non-linear patterns in the data, providing deeper and more accurate insights.

Investment in Data Skills: Organizations have been investing in data competencies, including the formation of data science teams and the implementation of robust data infrastructure. This investment has allowed organizations to explore the full potential of Big Data, transforming raw data into actionable insights that can inform strategic decisions.

In the online advertising landscape, data science plays a monumental role. It enables advertisers to:

Advanced Segmentation: Segment the audience more precisely based on a wide variety of criteria, ensuring the right messages reach the right people at the right time.

Real-Time Optimization: Adjust campaigns in real-time based on performance and user feedback, allowing for continuous optimization and better ROI. Data science also brought the ability to predict trends and optimize campaigns for future performance. Advanced algorithms can now predict how different audience segments might react to certain advertising messages, allowing advertisers to proactively adjust their strategies.

Performance Analysis: Evaluate campaign performance with unprecedented accuracy, identifying exactly what works, what doesn't, and why. Performance metrics have become more sophisticated with data science. It is now possible to track a myriad of metrics, from exposure and engagement to conversion and retention. This deep analysis allows for more accurate ROI assessment and informs campaign optimization strategies.

Programmatic Advertising: Utilize algorithms to automate ad space purchasing and optimize ad delivery.

Data science will continue to evolve, with new techniques, algorithms, and technologies emerging every day. To maintain relevance and competitiveness, organizations and advertising professionals will need to continuously invest in skills, technologies, and data infrastructure.

3 THE DATA JOURNEY

The data journey in the advertising industry is a fascinating narrative of transformation and insight. From the initial collection to in-depth analysis, each step of the journey is crucial for creating more effective and engaging advertising campaigns. Let's explore how data is collected, processed, and analyzed in the realm of online advertising.

3.1 Data Collection

Data collection is the starting point. Data can be collected from various sources:

Primary Data:

Collected directly from the target audience through online interactions, such as website visits, ad clicks, filled-out forms, among others. The collection of primary data is crucial as it provides direct and current insights into the audience's behavior and preferences. This can be done through various techniques, including tracking cookies, tracking pixels, and online forms.

- Tracking Cookies: Cookies are small text files that are stored in the user's browser and allow the tracking of visits and user activities on the site.
- Tracking Pixels: Pixels are small blocks of code embedded in a website that, when triggered, can send information back to a server about the user's activity.
- Online Forms: Online forms are a direct way to collect user information, such as name, email, preferences, among others.

Secondary Data:

These are pre-existing data, collected by third parties, such as market analysis companies or social media platforms. Secondary data can provide valuable context that helps better understand the market and your brand's position within that market.

- Market Analysis: Specialized companies can offer market analysis reports that include information on market trends, consumer behavior, and competitive analyses.
- Social Media Data: Social media platforms are a rich source of secondary data, offering insights into what consumers are saying and feeling about different brands and products.

Third-party Data:

Data purchased or acquired from external sources that aggregate information from various other sources. These data can be used to enrich primary and secondary data, providing a more holistic and comprehensive view.

- Demographic Databases: Provide information about the audience's demographics, which can be used for segmentation and personalization.

- Consumer Behavior Databases: Offer insights into how different consumer segments behave online and offline.

Effective data collection is the foundation upon which successful advertising strategies are built. With a clear understanding of where and how to collect relevant data, advertisers can begin to unravel the insights that will drive their campaigns to success.

3.2 Data Processing

After collection, the data goes through a cleaning and transformation process to ensure they are accurate and relevant. This is a crucial stage, as the data quality directly impacts the accuracy of the insights generated. The data processing process is often subdivided into three main steps: Cleaning, Transformation, and Enrichment.

Data Cleaning:

Data cleaning is the first essential step in data processing. It involves identifying and correcting or removing errors and inconsistencies in the data to improve quality and accuracy. Cleaning can include tasks such as:

- Typo Correction: Correcting spelling or typing errors in the data.
- Handling Missing Values: Filling in or deleting missing values in the data.
- Removal of Duplicates: Identifying and removing duplicate entries.
- Data Normalization: Standardizing data formats to ensure consistency.

```
import pandas as pd
df = pd.read_csv('dados_brutos.csv')
df = df.drop_duplicates()
df = df.fillna(method='ffill')
```

```
df['coluna'] = df['coluna'].str.replace('eror',
'error')
```

Data Transformation

Transformation involves converting raw data into a format more suitable for analysis. This may involve changing the data type, creating new columns from existing ones, or reorganizing the data.

- Creating New Columns: Deriving new columns based on existing ones.
- Data Type Change: For example, converting a string column to datetime.
- Data Reorganization: Such as pivoting tables to improve the data structure for analysis.
-

```
df['nova_coluna'] = df['coluna1'] + df['coluna2']
df['data'] = pd.to_datetime(df['data'])
df_pivot = df.pivot(index='ID', columns='variável',
values='valor')
```

Data Enrichment

Data enrichment is the process of combining different data sets to create a more complete profile. This may involve joining tables based on common keys or incorporating third-party data.

- Table Joining: Combining data from different tables based on a common key.
- Third-Party Data Incorporation: Incorporating demographic or consumer behavior data from external sources.

```
demografia_df = pd.read_csv('demografia.csv')
df_enriquecido = pd.merge(df, demografia_df,
on='ID')
```

Through cleaning, transformation, and enrichment, advertisers can refine the collected data into a valuable resource for analysis and insight. This meticulous data processing is the foundation for extracting meaningful information that can inform and guide effective advertising strategies.

3.3 Data Analysis

This is where the magic happens. Through advanced data science techniques, advertisers can extract valuable insights:

- Segmentation: Identification of distinct groups within an audience to allow message personalization.
- Predictive Modeling: Use of historical data to predict future consumer interactions.
- Sentiment Analysis: Understanding consumers' emotions and opinions regarding products or brands.
- Campaign Optimization: Analysis of campaign performance to make real-time adjustments.

3.4 Data Visualization

Visualization helps present insights in a clear and comprehensible manner, facilitating decision-making:

• Interactive Dashboards: Allow a clear view of campaign performance.

• Customized Reports: Tailored to the specific needs of different stakeholders.

• Insight Implementation: The insights derived from the data are then utilized to inform advertising strategies:

• Creation of Targeted Campaigns: Development of campaigns that resonate with different audience segments.

• Resource Allocation: Directing resources to channels and strategies that demonstrate a better return on investment.

• A/B Testing: Continuous experimentation to find the most effective messages and creatives.

The data journey is a continuous and iterative endeavor. As more data is collected and analyzed, and new technologies and analysis techniques are developed, the ability of advertisers to understand and engage their audience will continue to evolve. This journey, with its promise of increased efficacy and efficiency in online advertising, is a testament to the transformative power of data science in the advertising industry.

4 ALGORITHMS THAT POWER ADVERTISING

Online advertising has evolved into a highly technical and data-driven domain. At the heart of this evolution are algorithms and machine learning (ML) techniques that allow marketing professionals to better understand their audience and optimize their advertising campaigns. Let's explore some of the main algorithms and ML techniques employed in the advertising industry.

4.1 Audience Segmentation

Clustering Algorithms

Segmentation is a crucial task in advertising as it allows companies to target their messages to the most relevant consumer groups. Clustering algorithms, such as K-means and DBSCAN, are powerful tools in this regard as they can group individuals based on similar characteristics and behaviors.

K-means

The K-means algorithm is a popular clustering technique that attempts to find groups in data based on the mean of the values. The idea is simple: determine K initial centers, assign each point to the nearest center, and then recalculate the centers based on the mean of the assigned points.

```
from sklearn.cluster import KMeans
import pandas as pd
df = pd.read_csv('dados_do_publico.csv')
kmeans = KMeans(n_clusters=3, random_state=0).fit(df)
df['cluster'] = kmeans.labels_
```

DBSCAN

Unlike K-means, DBSCAN (Density-Based Spatial Clustering of Applications with Noise) does not require the number of clusters to be specified in advance. It operates on the concept of density, where a cluster is a dense area of points separated by areas of lower point density.

```
from sklearn.cluster import DBSCAN
dbscan = DBSCAN(eps=0.5, min_samples=5).fit(df)
df['cluster'] = dbscan.labels_
```

Evaluating the generated clusters is a crucial step in understanding audience segmentation. Methods like silhouette analysis can help assess the quality of clustering. Moreover, interpreting the clusters, through analyzing common characteristics within each cluster, is crucial for understanding the audience profile in each segment.

```
from sklearn.metrics import silhouette_score
score = silhouette_score(df.drop('cluster', axis=1),
df['cluster'])
```

```
print(f'Silhouette Score: {score}')
```

With audience segmentation accomplished, marketers can create more targeted advertising campaigns. For instance, they can direct specific ads to different demographic or behavioral groups identified in the clusters. Additionally, they can adjust ad messages to resonate better with the characteristics and behaviors of each group.

Audience segmentation is becoming increasingly sophisticated with the advent of new machine learning and big data techniques. More advanced algorithms and techniques like deep learning are being explored for more precise segmentation and identification of audience niches.

The ability to segment audiences more precisely and in real time is transforming the way advertising is done, allowing for unprecedented customization and, consequently, more effective and efficient advertising campaigns.

4.2 Click-Through Rate (CTR) Prediction

The Click-Through Rate (CTR) is a crucial metric in the domain of online advertising as it indicates the effectiveness of an advertising campaign. CTR prediction is the process of estimating the likelihood of a user clicking on an ad. This prediction is fundamental for optimizing resource allocation in advertising campaigns and improving ROI (Return on Investment).

Logistic Regression

Logistic Regression is a commonly used statistical technique for predicting the likelihood of a binary event, making it particularly suitable for CTR prediction, where the binary event is whether a user clicks on an ad or not.

Here is a simplified example of how logistic regression can be implemented to predict CTR:

```python
from sklearn.linear_model
import LogisticRegression
from sklearn.model_selection import train_test_split
from sklearn.preprocessing import StandardScaler
X, y = df.drop('clicou', axis=1), df['clicou']
X_train, X_test, y_train, y_test =
train_test_split(X, y, test_size=0.2,
random_state=42)
scaler = StandardScaler()
X_train = scaler.fit_transform(X_train)
X_test = scaler.transform(X_test)
lr = LogisticRegression()
lr.fit(X_train, y_train)
accuracy = lr.score(X_test, y_test)
print(f'Acurácia: {accuracy * 100:.2f}%')
```

The interpretation of the coefficients of logistic regression can provide insights into which features are most influential in predicting clicks. For example, a positive coefficient indicates that the corresponding feature increases the likelihood of a click, while a negative coefficient indicates the opposite.

```python
coef_df = pd.DataFrame(lr.coef_, columns=X.columns)
print(coef_df)
```

In the real world, CTR prediction can be much more complex, and other techniques and optimizations can be applied to improve the model's performance. For instance:

- Feature Engineering: Creating new features that may have a significant impact on CTR prediction.
- Ensemble Models: Combining the predictions of multiple models to obtain a more robust prediction.
- Deep Learning: Using deep neural networks that can capture complex interactions between features.

Besides logistic regression, other machine learning techniques can also be utilized for CTR prediction, such as:

- Decision Trees and Random Forest: These models can capture non-linear interactions between features and offer an intuitive graphical interpretation.
- Gradient Boosting Machines (like XGBoost or LightGBM): They are known for their high performance and ability to handle large and unbalanced datasets.

Thus, the ability to predict CTR allows advertisers to:

- Optimize Resource Allocation: Allocate budgets more efficiently to maximize engagement.
- Personalize Campaigns: Adapt advertising messages for specific audience segments that are more likely to click.
- Evaluate Campaign Performance: Monitor the effectiveness of advertising campaigns in real time and adjust strategies as needed.

With the continuous advancement of machine learning techniques and the growing availability of data, CTR prediction will continue to evolve. More sophisticated algorithms and the integration of real-time data can lead to more accurate predictions and more effective advertising strategies. Furthermore, the exploration of deep learning and reinforcement learning techniques presents new opportunities for innovation in CTR prediction and advertising campaign optimization.

4.3 Content Personalization

Content personalization is a crucial strategy in online advertising, as it helps to present the most relevant ads to users, increasing the likelihood of engagement.

Recommendation systems are the engine behind this personalization, allowing advertising platforms to offer ads that resonate with individual users' preferences and behaviors.

Recommendation systems use algorithms to predict a user's preference for an item or service. There are various approaches to building recommendation systems, with collaborative filtering and content-based filtering being the most common.

Collaborative filtering relies on interactions between users and items. It attempts to predict a user's preference for an item based on the preferences of other users with similar behaviors.

```
from surprise import KNNBasic
from surprise import Dataset
from surprise.model_selection import cross_validate
data = Dataset.load_builtin('ml-100k')
algo = KNNBasic()
cross_validate(algo, data, measures=['RMSE', 'MAE'],
cv=5, verbose=True)
```

Content-based filtering, on the other hand, uses the characteristics of the items and the user's profile to recommend items similar to those the user has shown interest in the past.

```
from sklearn.feature_extraction.text import
TfidfVectorizer
from sklearn.metrics.pairwise import linear_kernel
tfidf = TfidfVectorizer(stop_words='english')
tfidf_matrix = tfidf.fit_transform(df['descricao'])
cosine_sim = linear_kernel(tfidf_matrix,
tfidf_matrix)
```

There can also be hybrid systems that combine collaborative and content-based filtering to leverage the benefits of both approaches, offering more robust and accurate recommendations.

Content personalization has a direct impact on the effectiveness of advertising campaigns in the following ways:

- Ad Relevance: More relevant ads are more likely to engage users.

- User Experience: Personalization improves the user experience by showing ads that resonate with their preferences and behaviors.

- Advertising ROI: Personalization can lead to better return on investment, maximizing the efficiency of advertising campaigns.

This trend is becoming increasingly sophisticated with the advent of emerging technologies, such as Deep Learning, i.e., deep neural networks can capture complex patterns in the data, leading to more accurate recommendations; and Reinforcement Learning, which uses learning techniques to optimize personalization in real-time, adapting to user behavior over time.

The continuous evolution of recommendation systems and the integration of new technologies are opening new frontiers in content personalization, creating opportunities for more effective and engaging advertising campaigns. These innovations are defining the future of online advertising, where every interaction can be personalized to meet the unique preferences and needs of each user.

4.4 Real-Time Bidding (RTB)

Real-Time Bidding (RTB) optimization is a fundamental aspect of programmatic advertising, allowing advertisers to participate in real-time auctions to place their ads in available advertising spaces. Optimization algorithms play a crucial role in this process, helping advertisers determine how much to bid to maximize the probability of winning the auction while optimizing the return on investment (ROI). Subsequently, we will discuss some of these algorithms.

Upper Confidence Bound (UCB)

The Upper Confidence Bound algorithm is an action selection strategy aimed at balancing the exploration of lesser-known actions with the exploitation of known actions that have high rewards.

```
import numpy as np
mean_rewards = np.mean(rewards, axis=0)
upper_bound = mean_rewards + np.sqrt(2 *
np.log(np.sum(rewards)) / np.sum(rewards, axis=0))
optimal_strategy = np.argmax(upper_bound)
```

Thompson Sampling

Thompson Sampling is another algorithm that attempts to balance exploration with exploitation and is particularly effective when rewards are probabilistic.

```
import random
import scipy.stats as stats
beta_samples = [stats.beta(a=1+success, b=1+total-
success).rvs() for success, total in zip(successes,
totals)]
optimal_strategy = np.argmax(beta_samples)
```

Reinforcement learning algorithms like Q-Learning and Deep Q Networks (DQN) are also being explored to optimize real-time bids.

```
import numpy as np
Q_table = np.zeros([state_space, action_space])
alpha = 0.1
gamma = 0.99
    for episode in range(num_episodes):
        state = env.reset()
```

```
    done = False

    while not done:
        action = np.argmax(Q_table[state, :] +
np.random.randn(1, action_space) * (1. / (episode +
1)))
            next_state, reward, done, _ =
env.step(action)
            Q_table[state, action] = Q_table[state,
action] + alpha * (reward + gamma *
np.max(Q_table[next_state, :]) - Q_table[state,
action])
            state = next_state
```

Real-time bid optimization has several practical applications in the advertising industry, some of them are:

- ROI Maximization: Advertisers can optimize their bids to maximize the return on investment.
- Efficient Budget Allocation: Allows efficient budget allocation across different campaigns and channels.
- Competitiveness in Auctions: Helps advertisers remain competitive in highly contested auctions.

This practice is evolving further with the advent of more advanced technologies, such as automation, which is playing an increasingly large role, with platforms that can adjust bids in real-time based on a variety of factors.

The continuous innovation in optimization algorithms and the integration of deep learning and reinforcement learning are creating new opportunities for real-time bid optimization, making programmatic advertising more effective and efficient. Advertisers who adopt these advanced technologies are well-positioned to maximize the value of their advertising campaigns and gain a competitive advantage in the rapidly evolving digital advertising landscape.

4.5 Emotion Analysis

Emotion Analysis is a technique that utilizes natural language processing (NLP) to determine the opinion, sentiment, or emotion expressed in a text. It's a valuable tool for understanding the audience's perception of brands, products, or advertising campaigns. The insights obtained through Emotion Analysis can be used to inform marketing strategies, improve customer engagement, and optimize advertising campaigns.

Natural Language Processing (NLP) Techniques

NLP is the field of artificial intelligence (AI) focused on the interaction between computers and human language. It involves the application of algorithms to identify and extract information from natural text, with one of these applications being emotion classification.

Emotion classification is a common NLP task that involves categorizing texts based on the expressed sentiment, usually into categories like positive, negative, or neutral.

```python
from sklearn.feature_extraction.text import
TfidfVectorizer
from sklearn.linear_model import LogisticRegression
from sklearn.pipeline import Pipeline
from sklearn.model_selection import train_test_split
X_train, X_test, y_train, y_test =
train_test_split(df['texto'], df['sentimento'],
test_size=0.2, random_state=42)
pipeline = Pipeline([
    ('tfidf', TfidfVectorizer()),
    ('clf', LogisticRegression())
 ])
pipeline.fit(X_train, y_train)
accuracy = pipeline.score(X_test, y_test)
print(f'Acurácia: {accuracy * 100:.2f}%')
```

Besides emotion classification, aspect analysis can be used to understand which specific aspects of a product or service are being discussed positively or negatively.

Another type of application is topic analysis, which can be used to discover the main topics discussed in a body of text, which can be useful to understand the main themes in customer feedback or online discussions.

```
from sklearn.decomposition import
LatentDirichletAllocation
tfidf = TfidfVectorizer()
tfidf_matrix = tfidf.fit_transform(df['texto'])
lda = LatentDirichletAllocation(n_components=5,
random_state=42)
topics = lda.fit_transform(tfidf_matrix)
```

NLP can be applied in advertising with the purpose of obtaining important insights, such as:

- Consumer Insights: Understanding consumer feeling can help brands adjust their marketing and communication strategies.
- Brand Monitoring: Emotion analysis can be used to monitor brand perception over time.
- Campaign Optimization: Consumer feedback collected through emotion analysis can be used to optimize advertising campaigns.

It's important to emphasize that Deep Learning techniques are also expanding the capacities of feeling analysis, allowing for more precise analyses. Moreover, the ability to analyze emotions in different languages is crucial for global brands.

Emotion analysis will continue to evolve with the advancement of NLP and deep learning technologies, offering brands more precise and actionable insights about public perception.

4.6 Conversion Path Analysis

Conversion path analysis is crucial for understanding

how users interact with different touchpoints along their customer journey, from the first interaction to the final conversion. Through this analysis, it's possible to identify which channels and touchpoints are most effective in driving users to conversion, allowing for a more informed and effective resource allocation. For this, understanding attribution models is strictly necessary.

Attribution models are fundamental for understanding the relative value of different touchpoints along the conversion path. They help assign a value to each interaction a user has with different channels before performing a desired conversion, such as a purchase or sign-up.

The more traditional attribution models include:

- Last Click Attribution: Assigns the entire value of the conversion to the last touchpoint before the conversion.

- First Click Attribution: Assigns the entire value of the conversion to the first touchpoint in the customer journey.

- Linear Attribution: Distributes the conversion value equally among all touchpoints along the customer journey.

Advanced algorithms can be utilized to craft attribution models that more precisely reflect the value of different touchpoints. Thus, we can employ algorithm-based attribution models such as:

- Time-Decay Attribution: Assigns more value to the more recent touchpoints.

- Position-Based Attribution: Assigns more value to the touchpoints at the beginning and end of the customer journey, with less value assigned to touchpoints in the middle.

- Data-Driven Attribution (or Algorithmic Attribution): Uses algorithms to analyze historical data and determine the relative importance of different touchpoints.

```
from sklearn.ensemble import RandomForestRegressor
X, y = df.drop('conversao', axis=1), df['conversao']
rf = RandomForestRegressor()
rf.fit(X, y)
importances = rf.feature_importances_
```

From these applications, advertisers and entrepreneurs can garner valuable insights for:

- Budget Optimization: With a clear understanding of the value of different channels and touchpoints, advertisers can allocate their budget more effectively.

- Campaign Evaluation: Evaluate the performance of different campaigns and channels to understand what is contributing to conversions.

- Customer Journey Personalization: Adapt the customer journey based on insights on how different touchpoints impact conversion.

Conversion path analysis and attribution are rapidly growing areas in the field of digital advertising, with new techniques and technologies emerging to help brands better understand and optimize the customer journey.

These are just a few examples of the many algorithms and machine learning techniques that are reshaping the field of online advertising. Through the employment of these advanced technologies, advertisers can now operate at a level of precision and efficiency unprecedented, providing more relevant and engaging experiences for consumers while maximizing the return on investment in their campaigns.

5 CONNECTING DATA WITH ADVERTISING PERFORMANCE

The digital age has brought a revolution to the world of advertising, introducing the ability to collect and analyze data on an unprecedented scale. This wealth of data is a goldmine for marketers, allowing a deeper understanding of consumer behavior and the optimization of online advertising campaigns. This chapter explores how data is utilized to shape and optimize advertising performance.

5.1 Understanding the Consumer

Demographic and Psychographic Analysis

The collection and analysis of demographic and psychographic data are crucial steps in developing effective advertising strategies. These analyses provide a deep understanding of the profile and preferences of the target audience, enabling the creation of more resonant and personalized campaigns.

Demographic Breakdown

Age, Gender, and Location

Basic data such as age, gender, and location help to shape the message and design of the campaign, ensuring it is relevant and appealing to the target audience.

Education and Income

Information regarding the education level and income bracket of the audience can inform the type of language and offers that will resonate more.

Marital Status and Family Size

These data can help understand the needs and priorities of the audience, enabling more effective segmentation.

Psychographic Breakdown

Interests and Hobbies

Knowing the interests and hobbies of the audience, advertisers can create messages that resonate on a more personal level.

Values and Opinions

Understanding the values and opinions of the audience can help create an emotional connection, which is crucial for engagement and brand loyalty.

Lifestyle and Purchasing Behavior

Analyzing the lifestyle and purchasing behavior can provide insights on when and how the audience prefers to interact with brands.

Sentiment Analysis

Sentiment analysis is a powerful tool for understanding the public's perception of a brand or product. It can provide valuable feedback that can be used to adjust marketing and communication strategies.

Social Media Monitoring

Real-Time Feedback
Social media provides a steady stream of real-time feedback which, when analyzed, can provide insights into public sentiment.

Sentiment Trends and Crises
Identifying sentiment trends or emerging crises allows for a swift response, helping to maintain brand reputation.

Qualitative and Quantitative Analysis

Analysis Tools
There are several tools that can automate sentiment analysis, providing a quantitative view of public sentiment. Moreover, manual qualitative analysis can help understand the context and nuances of public feedback.

Continuous Improvement
Sentiment analysis should be an ongoing activity, with insights being used to inform and adjust marketing and communication strategies continuously.

Implications for Advertising Strategies

Content Development
Sentiment analysis can inform content development, ensuring messages resonate positively with the audience.

Crisis Management
In the event of a reputation crisis, sentiment analysis can provide valuable insights into public perception, helping to shape the brand's response.

The combination of demographic, psychographic, and sentiment analysis provides a solid foundation for creating and optimizing advertising campaigns. By understanding who the audience is and how they perceive the brand, advertisers are better positioned to develop strategies that resonate and engage effectively.

5.2 Segmentation and Personalization

Segmentation and personalization are two crucial strategies that have redefined how advertisers interact with audiences in the digital age. Both strategies are enabled by the availability and analysis of large volumes of data that can be collected in real-time and on an unprecedented scale.

Starting with audience segmentation, this strategy allows advertisers to break down a large audience into more manageable subgroups with common characteristics or behaviors. In the past, segmentation could be quite basic, perhaps focusing on obvious demographic variables like age and location. However, the advent of digital data has transformed this practice, allowing much more granular segmentation. Now, advertisers can segment audiences based on a wide range of criteria, including purchasing behavior, online interactions, social media preferences, and even web browsing patterns. For instance, it's possible to segment users who visited a specific site in the last 30 days, or who placed an item in their shopping cart but did not complete the purchase. This ability to segment so specifically means advertisers can create much more focused and relevant campaigns, increasing the chances of engagement and conversion.

However, segmentation is just the tip of the iceberg. Once an audience is segmented, the next step is to personalize the content served to these individuals. Personalization takes relevance to a new level, adjusting the advertising message to resonate with the unique characteristics and behaviors of each individual within a segment. For example, an ad for a product can be personalized based on the user's previous purchase history, or interactions they had with the brand's website. The possibilities are virtually endless, and machine learning and artificial intelligence techniques are making personalization more advanced every day.

Personalization is not limited only to the ad content itself, but extends to how the ad is delivered. For instance, data can inform the ideal time to serve an ad to an individual, or on what type of device they are more likely to interact with the ad. This can further extend to personalize the user's journey through a series of digital touchpoints, creating a truly integrated and personalized experience.

Both strategies, segmentation and personalization, are fueled by robust data analysis. Advertisers now have the ability to collect and analyze vast amounts of data in real-time, allowing for dynamic adjustments in segmentation and personalization strategies. This is a significant competitive advantage as it allows brands to react quickly to changes in consumer behavior or market conditions.

However, despite their advantages, segmentation and personalization also bring challenges. Data privacy is a growing concern among consumers, and regulations are evolving to ensure data is collected and used ethically. Additionally, the technical complexity involved in collecting, analyzing, and applying data for segmentation and personalization is significant, requiring a considerable investment in technology and skills.

Looking ahead, segmentation and personalization will continue to evolve, driven by ongoing advances in data technology and analysis. For advertisers, the ability to adapt to these changes and leverage the power of data will be crucial to maintaining relevance and competitiveness in a rapidly evolving digital environment.

5.3 Campaign Optimization

Campaign optimization is a fundamental practice to maximize the return on investment (ROI) in digital marketing. Optimization strategies have sharply evolved with the advancement of data technologies, allowing advertisers a deeper understanding and quicker reaction to real-time campaign dynamics.

A/B and Multivariate Testing

A widely recognized method for optimizing campaigns is A/B testing, where two or more versions of a page or ad are tested to determine which one performs better regarding a specific metric, be it the click-through rate, conversion rate, or any other relevant KPI. By creating two distinct versions of an ad, for example, and presenting them to the target audience, advertisers can collect data on which version is more effective in achieving the desired goal. This A/B testing practice is of immense value, as it helps understand what resonates with the audience and what doesn't, informing future decisions on design, content, and ad delivery strategy.

Beyond A/B testing, multivariate testing is an evolution that allows testing multiple variables simultaneously to determine the ideal combination that maximizes performance. In a multivariate test, several variables such as the headline, image, and call to action, can be tested in different combinations to understand how they interact with each other and which combination offers the best performance. This type of testing can reveal more complex insights and nuances that might be missed in a simpler A/B test.

Real-Time Performance Analysis

But campaign optimization doesn't end with A/B and multivariate testing. Real-time performance analysis is another cornerstone of modern campaign optimization. In the past, advertisers might have had to wait days or even weeks to collect and analyze campaign performance data. However, with today's technologies, data can be collected, analyzed, and acted upon in real-time. This allows advertisers to adjust their campaigns on-the-fly, whether changing the ad content, audience segmentation, or campaign budget, all in response to how the campaign is performing in real-time.

Real-time performance analysis is a powerful feature, as it allows advertisers to be more agile and reactive, adjusting their strategies to maximize ROI. For instance, if real-time analysis reveals that a campaign is performing poorly in a certain demographic segment, advertisers can readjust the segmentation or ad content to improve performance. Furthermore, if real-time analysis shows that a campaign is exceeding expectations during a particular period of the day, advertisers may choose to increase the campaign budget during that period to capitalize on that performance.

The combination of robust testing and real-time analysis creates a highly effective and data-driven campaign optimization approach. This approach allows advertisers to make the most out of their advertising budgets, ensuring that every dollar spent is contributing to achieving the campaign goals. As data technologies continue to evolve, it's likely we'll see even more advanced campaign optimization techniques emerge, providing advertisers with even greater opportunities to enhance campaign performance and maximize ROI.

5.4 ROI and Attribution Analysis

The analysis of Return on Investment (ROI) and attribution are crucial for understanding the effectiveness of advertising campaigns. As the consumer journey becomes increasingly complex with multiple digital touchpoints, precise understanding of campaign performance and budget optimization becomes vital for success in digital marketing.

Attribution models play a central role in this analysis. They help decipher the path consumers take from their first interaction with a brand to the final conversion, be it a purchase, a download, or any other desired action. The data collected along this journey is precious as it allows advertisers to understand which touchpoint had the most impact on the consumer's final decision. For example, was it the first ad seen, the follow-up email, or the final search on the brand's website that drove the conversion? Without a robust attribution model, answering these questions would be nearly impossible.

Various attribution models like linear attribution, time decay, and position-based attribution offer different ways of attributing value to the various touchpoints in the marketing funnel. Each of these models has its own advantages and disadvantages, and the right model choice may vary depending on the specifics of the campaign and business objectives.

Furthermore, a more precise analysis of ROI is achieved through these attribution models. By understanding how different touchpoints contribute to conversion, advertisers can calculate the return on investment more precisely, helping them understand the real value that each aspect of the campaign brings to the table.

With a clearer view of campaign performance comes the opportunity for budget optimization. Advertisers, armed with detailed insights about what's working and what's not, can allocate their budgets more effectively. For example, if a certain type of ad is generating a higher ROI, it makes sense to allocate more resources to that channel. Similarly, if a particular touchpoint is underperforming, it may be wise to redirect that budget to more productive areas.

Moreover, budget optimization is not a one-time action, but an ongoing process. With real-time data analysis, advertisers can monitor campaign performance in real-time and make on-the-fly budget adjustments to ensure they are maximizing ROI. For instance, if real-time analysis reveals that a campaign is exceeding expectations in a certain demographic or geographic segment, advertisers may choose to increase the budget to capitalize on that performance.

ROI and attribution analysis, therefore, is not just about looking back and understanding what worked; it's about using these insights to make informed decisions and optimize future performance. This data-driven approach to analysis and optimization is what allows advertisers to remain agile and competitive in a rapidly evolving digital marketing environment. By understanding past and current performance, and being ready to react to these insights in real-time, advertisers are well-positioned to maximize ROI, optimize the budget, and ultimately drive the long-term success of their online advertising campaigns.

5.5 Future Trends

The realm of online advertising is constantly evolving, driven by technological innovations that are reshaping the way advertisers interact with audiences. Among these innovations, Artificial Intelligence (AI) and Machine Learning (ML) are at the forefront, providing tools and insights that are elevating digital advertising to new heights.

AI and ML are enabling more sophisticated analyses as

they can process large volumes of data at a speed and accuracy that would be impossible for human analysts. These analyses can reveal patterns and insights that can be used to optimize advertising campaigns. For example, through the analysis of large data sets, ML algorithms can identify which attributes of an ad are correlated with higher click-through rates, or which audience segments are more likely to convert.

Moreover, AI and ML are facilitating automation at a level that was unimaginable until recently. Campaigns can be adjusted in real-time based on performance and user interactions, without the need for human intervention. This not only saves time and resources but can also lead to more effective optimization as algorithms can react instantly to changes in market conditions or user behavior.

Simultaneously, the digital advertising landscape is expanding beyond single-channel silos to encompass integrated campaigns across multiple channels and devices. Data-driven advertising across channels is a growing trend as advertisers recognize the need to reach consumers wherever they are, be it on desktop, mobile, or through social media platforms. Data analysis becomes crucial here as it can help advertisers understand how consumers interact with the brand across different channels and devices, and what the impact of these interactions is on conversion and engagement.

The ability to analyze and optimize campaigns across multiple channels is also fundamental to providing a cohesive user experience. Consumers today expect a consistent brand experience, regardless of the channel or device they are using. Data analysis can help advertisers understand how different touchpoints contribute to the consumer journey, and optimize message and ad delivery to provide an integrated and personalized experience.

These trends point towards a future where online advertising will be even more personalized, data-driven, and integrated across multiple channels and devices. AI and ML, along with robust data analysis, will be fundamental in driving this evolution, allowing advertisers to create more innovative and effective advertising strategies.

It's an exciting time for advertisers who are willing to embrace these new technologies and trends. Those who do so will be well-positioned to leverage emerging opportunities and reach consumers in new and engaging ways. In an increasingly competitive and saturated market, data-driven innovation will be the key to standing out and connecting with audiences in meaningful ways.

The connection between data and advertising performance is a powerful alliance that, when handled correctly, can transform the efficacy of online advertising campaigns. This chapter highlights the importance of data in optimizing advertising performance and explores the various ways in which data can be utilized to enhance digital advertising strategies.

6 PERSONALIZATION AND SCALE

Personalization is a phenomenon that has transformed the way brands interact with their audiences. In the realm of online advertising, personalization has transcended from a mere differentiator to a core consumer expectation. Behind this transformation are data, acting as the catalyst, enabling brands to create personalized advertising experiences that resonate with individuals on an unprecedented scale.

The magic of personalization in online advertising lies in the ability to treat each consumer as unique, delivering messages and offers that are highly relevant to their individual preferences, behaviors, and interaction history. This is achieved through the collection and analysis of a wealth of consumer data, allowing for granular segmentation and content personalization.

The breadth and depth of data available to advertisers today are astounding. From basic demographic data to detailed online behavior information, through purchase histories and social media interactions, advertisers have access to a wealth of information that can be used to personalize the advertising experience. And with the evolution of data collection and analysis technology, the ability to extract valuable insights and apply them in creating personalized advertising campaigns is only growing.

But, how is this done on the internet scale, where advertisers might be interacting with millions or even billions of consumers? The answer is through automation driven by artificial intelligence and machine learning. Advanced algorithms can process large volumes of data, identify patterns and audience segments, and automate the delivery of personalized content. This enables advertisers to personalize campaigns for large audiences with an efficiency and effectiveness that would be impossible manually.

Furthermore, recommendation systems, which are a form of personalization, use data to suggest products, services, or relevant content to users based on their past behavior and preferences. These systems are an example of how data can be utilized to create highly personalized advertising experiences that encourage engagement and conversion.

Upon a good understanding of the data, audience segmentation becomes a critical step. Segmenting the audience based on the collected information helps create distinct groups of consumers with similar characteristics or needs. This segmentation is vital for creating more effective personalization strategies.

With well-defined audience segments, content personalization is the next natural step. Developing content and offers that resonate with each audience segment is crucial. Personalization can range from creating specific products and offers to personalizing marketing messages and the user experience on the site or app.

To implement large-scale personalization, technology plays a crucial role. Investments in advanced content management systems, marketing automation platforms, and AI and machine learning technologies can automate many aspects of personalization, allowing brands to reach a broader audience with personalized messages. The effectiveness of personalization needs to be continuously assessed and optimized.

This can be done through A/B and multivariate testing, which help understand the impact of personalization strategies and identify areas of improvement. Customer feedback is also invaluable, providing direct insights on how personalization is perceived and what areas might need adjustments. Machine learning and AI not only facilitate the automation of personalization but also real-time optimization. These technologies can analyze consumer behavior in real-time and adjust personalization accordingly, ensuring that messages remain relevant and engaging.

Programmatic advertising is another vital aspect of large-scale personalization. It enables the automated delivery of personalized ads to specific audience segments in real-time, taking personalization to a new level.

Cross-channel integration is equally important to ensure that the customer experience is cohesive across all digital channels. An effective personalization strategy must ensure that the customer experience is consistent, no matter how or where a customer interacts with the brand.

Continuous monitoring and analysis are crucial to ensure that personalization strategies continue to deliver value. This involves ongoing performance analysis, adjusting strategies as necessary to ensure that personalization meets consumer expectations.

Last but not least, education and training are key to ensuring that the team has the knowledge and skills necessary to implement, manage, and optimize personalization strategies. This is a vital investment to ensure the ongoing success of personalization in digital businesses. By navigating through all these steps, brands can create robust personalized experiences that not only resonate with their customers but also drive the success of digital businesses in an increasingly competitive online environment.

Personalization at the internet scale is also creating a reset of consumer expectations. Consumers now expect brands to understand their needs and preferences and are disappointed with generic experiences. This shift in expectation is creating a sort of feedback loop, where successful personalization creates an expectation of personalization, which in turn drives greater data collection and analysis to meet these expectations.

The continuation of this trend suggests a future where personalization will be even more integrated and central to the online advertising experience. Advertisers who can leverage data to deliver large-scale personalization will be well-positioned to build stronger and lasting relationships with their audiences, and consequently, achieve better performance in their advertising campaigns.

However, along with these opportunities, comes the responsibility of managing data ethically and ensuring the privacy and security of consumer data. This is a critical aspect that advertisers will have to navigate as they embark on the journey of personalization at the internet scale.

7 METRICS ANALYSIS

In today's competitive digital environment, measuring the performance of advertising campaigns is crucial to understand the return on investment (ROI) and make informed decisions for future marketing strategies. At the center of this measurement are the metrics, which serve as quantifiable indicators of the performance and success of a campaign. Here are some of the critical metrics and how they can be analyzed to optimize the success of the campaign.

7.1 Click-Through Rate (CTR)

The Click-Through Rate (CTR), by revealing the ratio of clicks to views, is a direct indicator of an ad's resonance with its target audience. A higher CTR suggests that the ad is relevant and appealing, while a lower CTR may indicate the need for optimizations. The practical analysis of CTR can occur on several layers, depending on the desired level of depth.

An initial practical method is the direct comparison of CTRs between different ads within the same campaign or among different campaigns. This is a quick method to identify which ads are outperforming others and, possibly, why. For example, an ad with a clear message and an attractive call to action may have a higher CTR compared to an ad with a confusing message.

Beyond direct comparison, a deeper analysis may involve segmenting the CTR by different demographics or user behaviors. For example, analyzing how the CTR varies among different age groups, geographies, or devices can provide insights into how the ad message resonates with different audience segments. This segmented analysis can help identify opportunities to customize ads for different audience segments and improve the overall effectiveness of the campaign.

A/B testing is another valuable method for analyzing CTR. For example, creating two versions of an ad with different calls to action or images and comparing the CTR can help understand which elements of the ad are more appealing to the audience. A/B tests can be conducted in several rounds, each building on the learnings from the previous round, to continuously and iteratively optimize CTR.

Furthermore, trend analysis over time is important. Monitoring how an ad or campaign's CTR changes over time can help identify trends and possibly correlate changes in CTR with changes in campaign strategy or market environment.

Lastly, analyzing CTR in conjunction with other metrics, such as cost per click (CPC) and conversion rate (CVR), can provide a more holistic view of ad performance. For example, an ad with a high CTR but low CVR may indicate that, although the ad is appealing, it may not be leading to desired actions, necessitating adjustments to the landing page or ad message.

The practical application of these analysis methods can offer advertisers valuable insights on how to improve the effectiveness of their campaigns and optimize performance to achieve their marketing goals.

7.2 Cost Per Click (CPC)

Practical analysis of Cost Per Click (CPC) is fundamental to keep track of the financial performance of online advertising campaigns. CPC is a direct metric that influences both customer acquisition cost and the return on investment (ROI) of campaigns. Appreciating CPC in a contextual manner and acting based on this appreciation can bring significant improvements to a campaign's performance.

One of the first practical activities in CPC analysis is to monitor its evolution over time. Observing how CPC changes daily or weekly can help identify trends. For example, an increase in CPC may indicate fiercer competition in the ad auction, while a decrease may suggest an opportunity to gain quality traffic at a lower cost.

Adjusting bids is a central activity in managing CPC. For instance, if the goal is to reduce acquisition cost, then lowering the bid might be a viable strategy. However, it's important to note that a lower bid may result in fewer impressions and, possibly, less traffic. Therefore, finding a balance between the bid and desired performance is crucial.

A deeper analysis of CPC may involve comparing CPC across different campaigns, ad groups or even individual ads. This can help identify which campaigns or ads are getting a better return on investment and which may need optimization.

Furthermore, examining CPC along with other metrics such as Click-Through Rate (CTR) and Conversion Rate (CVR) can provide a more holistic view. For example, a low CPC with a high CTR may be indicative of a successful campaign, while a high CPC with a low CVR may indicate problems that need addressing.

The use of automated tools for bid management is also

a common practice to optimize CPC. Online advertising platforms often offer bid optimization tools that can automatically adjust bids based on a desired CPC or ROI objective. In addition, advanced techniques like algorithm-based automated bidding can be utilized to further optimize CPC.

CPC is also often analyzed in relation to the customer lifetime value (CLV). This can help understand if the customer acquisition cost is aligned with the value these customers bring over time.

Continuous analysis and optimization of CPC are essential activities that can help advertisers maximize the return on their advertising investments, while simultaneously ensuring they are reaching their target audiences effectively and efficiently. By understanding CPC in a broader context and applying practical strategies for its analysis and optimization, advertisers can make more informed use of their advertising budgets and improve the performance of their campaigns.

7.3 Conversion Rate (CVR)

The Conversion Rate (CVR) plays a central role in evaluating the performance of an online advertising campaign. A high CVR indicates that a significant number of users who clicked on the ad performed the desired action, be it a purchase, a registration, or any other defined conversion goal. On the other hand, a low CVR may signal problems that need attention, such as an unappealing landing page or an irrelevant ad.

A practical first step in analyzing the CVR is to observe the rate over time. A temporal analysis can reveal trends, and spikes or drops in the CVR can be correlated with changes in the campaign or market environment. Additionally, comparing the CVR among different campaigns, ad groups or individual ads can help identify which are more effective in converting users.

The analysis of the landing page is crucial to understanding the CVR. A well-designed landing page that resonates with the target audience and has a clear and appealing call to action can significantly improve the CVR. Analyzing the user experience on the landing page, such as the time spent on the page, the bounce rate, and the interaction with page elements, can provide valuable insights. Analytical tools and conversion tracking tools can help collect and analyze this data.

A/B testing is a powerful tool for improving CVR. Different versions of a landing page or ad can be tested to see which version has the best conversion rate. Tests may include changes in ad texts, landing page design, call to action positioning, among others. The learning obtained through continuous A/B testing can be used to make iterative improvements.

Furthermore, audience segmentation can be analyzed alongside the CVR. For example, analyzing how the CVR varies among different demographic or geographic segments can help understand how different groups respond to the ads and the landing page. This can, in turn, inform segmentation and personalization strategies to improve the CVR.

The relevance of the ad is another critical factor for CVR. If the ad is highly relevant to the target audience, they are more likely to perform the desired action after clicking. Ad relevance analyses and user feedback can help evaluate and improve the relevance of the ads.

Lastly, multichannel and multiplatform analysis can be beneficial. Understanding how different channels and platforms contribute to the CVR can inform a more holistic and integrated marketing strategy.

Practical and continuous analysis of the CVR, along with the implementation of optimization strategies based on the insights obtained, can significantly improve the performance of an online advertising campaign, contributing to a better ROI and a deeper understanding of audience behavior and preferences.

7.4 Cost-Per-Acquisition (CPA)

Cost-Per-Acquisition (CPA) is a crucial financial metric that provides a clear view of an advertising campaign's economic efficiency. Simply put, CPA represents the cost of acquiring a new customer. This metric is vital for any business investing in advertising, as a high CPA can quickly erode margins, while a low CPA may indicate an opportunity to scale the campaign to acquire more customers at a reasonable cost.

One of the most common practical analyses is comparing the CPA with the Customer Lifetime Value (CLV). This comparison allows advertisers to see if the cost of acquiring a new customer is justified by the value that this customer will bring over time. If the CPA is significantly lower than the CLV, the campaign can be considered economical. On the other hand, a CPA that exceeds the CLV may indicate that the advertising strategy needs to be reviewed.

The analysis of CPA can also be done alongside other performance metrics such as Conversion Rate (CVR) and Cost-Per-Click (CPC). For instance, a high CPA with a low CVR may indicate that although users are clicking on the ads, few are converting, which might signal a problem with the landing page or the ad's relevance. Similarly, a high CPA with a high CPC might suggest that advertising costs are too high.

A practical way to analyze and optimize the CPA is through bid adjustments in pay-per-click (PPC) advertising campaigns. For example, if the CPA is too high, reducing the bids might help lower the acquisition cost. However, this should be done carefully, as lower bids might result in fewer impressions and possibly less traffic.

Furthermore, segmentation analysis can reveal valuable insights about CPA. For instance, different audience segments may have different CPAs, and understanding this can help optimize segmentation to focus on segments that are more economical to acquire.

Continuous optimization of the landing page and ad creatives can also have a significant impact on CPA. Improvements on the landing page that increase the conversion rate or more appealing ads that improve the CTR can, in turn, reduce the CPA.

In today's digital landscape, advanced analysis tools allow for deep analysis of CPA, including cohort analysis, where advertisers can see how CPA varies over time for different groups of customers acquired at different times. This can help understand the long-term effectiveness of advertising campaigns.

Moreover, competitive analysis can be valuable. Understanding how the CPA compares with industry standards or competitors can provide valuable context.

Practical analysis and continuous optimization of CPA are essential to ensure that advertising campaigns not only attract new customers but do so in a way that is financially sustainable and beneficial for the business in the long term. By understanding how CPA relates to other key metrics and the overall campaign performance, advertisers can make informed decisions that improve ROI and contribute to the long-term success of their online advertising strategies.

7.5 Return on Advertising Spend (ROAS)

Return on Advertising Spend (ROAS) is a crucial metric that helps advertisers understand the efficacy of their advertising campaigns. This metric is calculated by dividing the revenue generated by advertising by the cost of advertising. For example, if you spent $1000 on advertising and generated $5000 in sales from that advertising, the ROAS would be 5. This is a simple yet powerful metric that gives a clear view of the return on advertising investment.

Evaluating ROAS across different channels and campaigns is a sagacious practice that can reveal where advertising money is being well spent and where it is not. For example, if a campaign on Facebook is generating a ROAS of 6, while a campaign on Google Ads is generating a ROAS of 2, it might be wise to reallocate more of the advertising budget to Facebook.

Furthermore, a detailed analysis of ROAS can help better understand how different elements of the campaign are contributing to the return. This includes the analysis of different ad groups, keywords, audience segments, and creatives. For instance, perhaps a certain ad group is performing very well, while another is not. This analysis can inform future decisions on where to focus advertising efforts and budget.

It's also beneficial to evaluate ROAS over time. This can help identify trends, like a declining ROAS that may signal a problem that needs to be addressed. Likewise, an increase in ROAS may indicate a successful improvement in advertising strategy.

Advanced advertising analysis tools can provide a deeper insight into ROAS, allowing for more granular analysis. For example, there could be the possibility to analyze ROAS on a very detailed level, such as the performance of different ad variations or how ROAS varies by device or geographical location.

An important aspect to consider is that while a positive ROAS is good, it should not be viewed in isolation. For instance, if the ROAS is good but the sales volume is very low, this might indicate that although the advertising is effective in terms of ROI, scale may be a problem.

Additionally, it's important to compare ROAS with other financial and performance metrics such as Cost-Per-Acquisition (CPA) and Customer Lifetime Value (CLV). A holistic analysis that includes various metrics can provide a more complete understanding of campaign performance.

In today's competitive environment, optimizing ROAS is crucial to ensure advertising dollars are being spent effectively. With careful and continuous analysis of ROAS, along with strategic adjustments based on acquired insights, advertisers can maximize the return on their advertising campaigns, ensuring that every dollar spent on advertising contributes to the growth and success of the business. This, in turn, can lead to a more effective advertising strategy and sustainable growth in the long term.

7.6 Social Media Engagement

Social Media Engagement is a vital metric for understanding how much an advertising campaign is resonating with the target audience. Measures of engagement, such as likes, shares, comments, and other interactions, are tangible indicators of a campaign's effectiveness in capturing attention and stimulating a response from the audience. These metrics are especially critical in the digital age, where competition for audience attention is fierce and direct interaction with the audience can be a significant differentiator.

Engagement analysis begins with collecting and monitoring these interaction metrics on relevant social media platforms. For example, if a campaign is being run on Facebook, Instagram, and Twitter, it would be prudent to monitor and analyze engagement metrics across all these platforms to get a holistic view of campaign performance.

When analyzing engagement, it is useful to compare the performance between different posts or ads. This can help identify what type of content is generating more engagement. For example, perhaps posts with images generate more likes and shares, while posts with videos generate more comments. These insights can be valuable for optimizing future content strategies.

Furthermore, engagement analysis can be enriched

when correlated with other performance metrics like website traffic, conversions, or sales. For instance, analysis might reveal that an increase in social media engagement correlates with an increase in website traffic or conversions. This can indicate that the campaign is not only capturing attention but also encouraging the desired action.

Beyond standard engagement metrics, advanced social media analysis tools can provide deeper insights, such as the reach and impression of a post, or the demographics and interests of the engaged audience. These additional analyses can help better understand the audience and fine-tune the campaign's message and content for better resonance and engagement.

Temporal analysis of engagement is also beneficial. For example, monitoring engagement over time can help identify trends or patterns, like an increase in engagement during certain times of the day or days of the week, or a shift in engagement in response to adjustments in content strategy.

A recommended practice is also to observe and analyze competitor engagement. This can provide a useful benchmark and perhaps reveal opportunities to improve engagement by observing what's working well for others in the industry.

Social media engagement analysis, therefore, is not just about monitoring likes, shares, and comments, but about delineating actionable insights that can be used to optimize content and advertising strategy. Through careful and continuous analysis of engagement, advertisers can adjust their campaigns for better resonance with the audience, resulting in higher engagement and, ultimately, better campaign outcomes.

Customer satisfaction and feedback are crucial indicators of the effectiveness of an advertising campaign. They offer a window into the audience's perception and response to a campaign's content, providing a valuable opportunity for advertisers to adjust and refine their strategies. Collecting and analyzing customer feedback is not only a way to measure campaign performance, but also a means to engage the audience and show that their opinions are valued.

Collecting customer feedback can be done in several ways. Online surveys, feedback forms on websites, comment sections on social media, and review platforms are all effective channels for collecting customer opinions. Additionally, sentiment analysis tools can be used to analyze online comments and reviews to gain a deeper understanding of customer sentiment towards a brand or product.

When analyzing feedback, it's important to not only observe positive comments but also pay special attention to negative feedback. Negative comments can provide critical insights into areas of improvement. For example, if several customers mention a specific aspect of a product that did not meet their expectations, this can signal an area that requires attention.

Utilizing customer feedback to make continuous adjustments in campaigns is a smart practice that can lead to significant improvements in both customer satisfaction and campaign performance. For example, if customer feedback indicates that an advertising message is unclear or misinterpreted, this may be an indication to review the ad content for better clarity and effectiveness.

Furthermore, customer feedback can be used to identify opportunities for more effective customization and segmentation. For example, if a particular segment of customers expresses appreciation for a particular type of offer or promotion, this can be used to tailor future campaigns to that segment.

Customer feedback can also be a powerful tool for creating testimonials and case studies that can be used in future advertising campaigns. Testimonials from satisfied customers can be extremely persuasive to potential customers.

Lastly, it's important to communicate back to customers that their feedback is valued and is being used to make improvements. This not only helps build trust and loyalty but also encourages continuous feedback, creating a cycle of continuous improvement that can lead to more effective advertising campaigns and greater customer satisfaction.

Therefore, customer satisfaction and feedback are not only performance metrics, but also valuable resources that can be utilized to optimize campaigns, improve customer satisfaction, and ultimately drive campaign performance to new heights. By adopting a customer-centric approach to campaign performance analysis, advertisers can cultivate a stronger relationship with their audience, while continuously refining and improving their advertising strategies.

These metrics, when analyzed correctly, can provide a wealth of information on campaign performance, allowing for informed adjustments and continuous optimization to meet and exceed marketing goals.

8 INTEGRATING DATA INTO ADVERTISING STRATEGIES

Integrating data into advertising strategy is a journey that begins with establishing a data-centric culture within the marketing team. This can be achieved through organizing training sessions on data analysis and relevant analytical tools like Google Analytics or Tableau. Regular workshops are also essential, where team members can share data insights and discuss how these insights can be applied in campaigns.

The next practical step is the implementation of data management platforms. Choosing a platform like Salesforce or Microsoft Dynamics that meets your organization's needs is crucial. Once the platform is selected, it's important to integrate data from different sources like CRM, social media, and Google Ads to have a unified view that can be used to make informed decisions.

With a robust data structure in place, marketers can start utilizing data in campaign creation. Audience segmentation using demographic and behavioral data is an effective way to ensure the right messages reach the right people. For example, segmentation tools in Facebook Ads can be used to target ads based on location, interests, and behaviors. Additionally, conducting A/B testing on different ad versions can help discover which messages resonate better with the audience.

Monitoring and real-time optimization are facilitated with the creation of real-time dashboards using tools like Google Data Studio. These dashboards allow advertisers to see campaign performance live and adjust bids in PPC campaigns in real time, ensuring that return on investment is optimized.

Moreover, collecting and analyzing customer feedback is vital to understand campaign effectiveness. Distributing customer satisfaction surveys via email or on social media and utilizing sentiment analysis tools to evaluate customer feedback on social media are practical ways to collect valuable insights.

Investing in emerging technology like AI-based automation solutions, such as chatbots for customer service, can free up time to focus on higher strategies. Multichannel analysis is also crucial, utilizing analytical tools to assess campaign performance across different channels and adjust budget allocation as necessary.

Finally, continuous data-based evaluation is vital. Conducting regular campaign reviews and adjusting the strategy as needed to improve performance is a practice that should be incorporated into the campaign management lifecycle. By following these practical steps, marketers can effectively integrate data into the advertising strategy, optimizing campaign performance, and ultimately achieving their business goals.

9 GET READY FOR THE FUTURE: DATA-DRIVEN MARKETING

The future of advertising is inextricably intertwined with data science. As we move towards an increasingly digitized world, the need to understand and interpret large volumes of data becomes ever more crucial. In this context, data-driven advertising is not just a competitive advantage, but a strategic necessity.

9.1 Adapting to Technological Change

The digital landscape is constantly evolving, with new platforms, technologies, and channels emerging at a breakneck pace. Adopting a mindset of continuous learning and being open to innovation is crucial to stay relevant and effective in the advertising space. This evolution is not just about keeping up with the latest tools or platforms, but about understanding how these changes can be leveraged to create more effective advertising campaigns. For example, the rise of social media led to new forms of advertising, such as influencer marketing and native ads. Similarly, the growing prevalence of data analysis technologies now allows for more precise audience segmentation and ad personalization on a scale never seen before. As the digital environment continues to evolve, marketers will need to keep learning and adapting to ensure their strategies remain effective.

9.2 Empowerment in Data Science

Mastery of data science is a core competency for modern marketing professionals. Training in data analysis, machine learning, and AI will aid in making more informed decisions, personalizing campaigns, and measuring performance more accurately. To truly integrate data science into advertising strategy, it is crucial that marketers not only have a basic understanding of these technologies but also know how to apply them practically. For example, understanding how to use machine learning algorithms to analyze large sets of consumer data can help identify patterns and insights that can be used to optimize advertising campaigns. Moreover, data science can be used to test and measure the effectiveness of different strategies, allowing for continuous optimization and better resource allocation. Empowerment in data science is not just about acquiring technical skills, but also about developing an analytical mindset that can help drive more informed and strategic decision-making in the advertising domain.

9.3 Investing in Analytical Tools

Advanced analytical tools have the power to transform large datasets into actionable insights that can be the foundation for strategic advertising decisions. Investing in such tools is an essential step for any marketing professional wishing to adopt a data-driven approach. For instance, data analysis tools can help understand user behavior, identify market trends, evaluate campaign effectiveness, and more.

Besides merely acquiring these tools, it's crucial to integrate them with the existing campaign management systems to create a cohesive digital ecosystem. Successful integration allows smooth data transfer between different platforms, providing a more holistic and actionable view of advertising campaigns. For instance, integrating a campaign management platform with a data analysis tool can enable real-time analysis of campaign performance, allowing quick and informed adjustments to maximize ROI.

In a practical scenario, consider a company that invested in an advanced data analysis tool. With this tool, they can segment their target audience more precisely by analyzing user behavior on their website and other digital platforms. Moreover, they can use predictive analysis to anticipate market trends and adjust their advertising strategies accordingly. With successful integration, the collected data can be easily transferred and utilized in their campaign management platform, enabling the execution of more informed and effective advertising campaigns.

Furthermore, continuous training is vital to ensure teams can effectively utilize these tools. Regular training and workshops can help teams stay updated on best practices and new features of analytical tools.

Lastly, when selecting and investing in analytical tools, it's important to consider not only their current capabilities but also their ability to adapt and evolve with the changing needs of the company and emerging industry trends. A platform that offers regular updates, robust technical support, and a strong user community can be an invaluable resource for marketers wishing to stay at the forefront of data-driven advertising.

9.4 Data-Driven Decision-Making Culture

Cultivating a culture of data-driven decision-making is a

fundamental step for organizations wishing to maximize the impact of their advertising strategies. It's a journey that goes beyond merely implementing tools and technologies but extends to promoting an analytical mindset among team members. In this culture, every strategic choice is grounded in insights derived from concrete data, rather than intuitions or assumptions.

One way to promote this culture is through continuous education and training. Offering workshops and training sessions on data analysis and interpretation can equip team members with the necessary knowledge to make informed decisions. Moreover, creating an environment where curiosity is encouraged can lead to valuable discoveries, encouraging team members to explore available data to better understand consumer behavior and campaign performance.

Besides training, the practice of data-driven decision-making can be incorporated into daily processes. For example, strategy meetings can be structured around campaign performance analyses, with discussions guided by insights derived from data. Additionally, creating accessible dashboards that display key metrics in real-time can serve as a constant reminder of the value of data.

Leadership also plays a critical role in cultivating this culture. When leaders demonstrate a commitment to data-driven decision-making, it sets an example for the entire organization. Leaders can demonstrate this commitment through regular communication about the importance of data, celebrating data-driven wins, and supporting initiatives that promote analytical competency within the organization.

Transparency is another crucial component. By sharing insights and analysis results with the team, organizations can promote a deeper understanding of the value that data can bring. This also includes being open about failures or unexpected findings, which are valuable learning opportunities.

Implementing technologies that facilitate data collection, analysis, and sharing is another practical step to promote a culture of data-driven decision-making. This may include investing in data analysis platforms, visualization tools, and campaign management systems that easily integrate with analytical solutions.

By aligning technology with a data analysis mindset and a commitment to education and transparency, organizations can develop a robust culture of data-driven decision-making. This, in turn, can lead to more effective advertising strategies, enabling companies to navigate confidently in the evolving digital landscape.

9.5 Collaboration and Strategic Partnerships

Collaboration and strategic partnerships are essential to accelerate digital transformation in advertising. By joining forces with technological partners, data platforms and other stakeholders, organizations can expedite access to valuable insights, advanced technologies and expertise that may not be available internally. This is a practical way to quickly absorb the innovations that are shaping data-driven advertising.

A practical way to start is by identifying and establishing partnerships with tech companies at the forefront of data science and analytics. These partnerships can provide access to advanced analytical tools, as well as the technical expertise needed to interpret and act on the data. For example, working with a data analysis platform can provide marketing teams with deeper insights into consumer behavior, allowing for more precise audience segmentation and more effective advertising campaigns.

Furthermore, partnerships can open doors to larger data pools that can be explored for valuable insights. For example, a partnership with a social media platform can provide access to demographic and behavioral data that can be used to refine segmentation and targeting strategies.

Collaborations can also be internal. Creating cross-functional teams composed of marketing, IT, data analytics and other relevant functions can promote a culture of collaboration and innovation. These teams can work together to identify opportunities, test new strategies, and share learnings.

It is equally important to foster an open environment for learning and experimentation. Encouraging teams to test new approaches, learn from the results, and iterate based on these learnings can lead to innovations that drive advertising performance.

Moreover, on the journey of collaboration, it is essential to establish effective communication channels with partners and stakeholders. Sharing objectives, success metrics, and feedback regularly can help align strategies and optimize the value derived from these partnerships.

Another practical aspect is participation in industry consortia or working groups focused on digital advertising and data science. These forums can provide opportunities to learn from peers, discover best practices, and explore new technologies and methodologies that can be applied to improve advertising campaign performance.

By investing in strategic partnerships and collaborations, either externally or internally, organizations are better positioned to navigate the digital evolution of advertising and leverage the opportunities presented by data science to enhance their advertising strategies and achieve their business goals.

9.6 Assessment and Optimization with Data-Driven Marketing

The dynamic nature of online advertising demands a continuous assessment and optimization approach. In an environment where consumer preferences, market trends, and advertising platform algorithms are constantly changing, the effectiveness of advertising campaigns can fluctuate. Therefore, adopting a proactive stance on assessment and continuous adjustments is crucial to keep campaign performance at an optimal level.

A practical way to incorporate continuous assessment and optimization is through the implementation of real-time performance dashboards that can provide immediate insights into campaign performance. These dashboards can be set up to monitor key metrics such as Click-Through Rate (CTR), Cost Per Click (CPC), Conversion Rate, among others. With this information at hand, marketing professionals can quickly identify areas for improvement and make informed decisions to optimize campaigns.

Automation is another crucial element in this journey of continuous assessment and optimization. Using marketing automation platforms that can adjust ad bids in real time, for example, can help maximize campaign ROI. These platforms can be programmed to adjust bids based on predefined criteria, freeing up marketing professionals to focus on higher-level strategies.

Predictive analytics can also play a vital role in continuous optimization. By analyzing historical patterns of campaign performance and market data, predictive models can provide projections on how different variables might impact future campaign performance. These insights can, in turn, inform optimization strategies, helping to allocate resources more effectively and adjust segmentation and content strategies to better resonate with the target audience.

Furthermore, it's important to foster a culture of A/B and multivariate testing to explore different versions of ads, landing pages, and segmentation strategies. By measuring the performance of different versions, valuable insights can be gained on what resonates better with the audience, thus making informed adjustments to improve campaign effectiveness.

Lastly, customer feedback and social media sentiment

analysis can provide an additional layer of insights for continuous optimization. By understanding how consumers are reacting to campaigns and the advertised products or services, marketing professionals can make more informed adjustments to improve resonance and ultimately campaign performance.

Through a systematic and data-driven approach to continuous assessment and optimization, marketing professionals can not only maintain campaign performance but also discover new opportunities for innovation and improve the ROI of their advertising activities.

Embracing data science in advertising is a commitment to excellence, innovation, and continuous value delivery to customers. As we move forward, the ability to interpret and act on data will not just be a facilitator of success but a critical necessity. By equipping themselves with the right competencies, tools, and mindset, marketing professionals are not just preparing for the future of data-driven advertising, but actively shaping it.

10 FUTURE TRENDS OF DATA-DRIVEN MARKETING

The online advertising landscape has been witnessing continual evolution with the introduction of emerging technologies. Among these, Artificial Intelligence (AI), Augmented Reality (AR), and Blockchain are shaping the future of advertising, promoting a significant transformation in the way campaigns are created, managed, and evaluated.

AI, with its ability to process large volumes of data and extract valuable insights, is playing a central role in automating and optimizing advertising campaigns. For instance, through machine learning, AI algorithms can analyze consumer behavior and adjust ads in real-time to better cater to audience preferences and behaviors. Moreover, AI is facilitating the creation of personalized advertising content, helping brands create more resonant and relevant messages.

On the other hand, AR is providing advertisers an innovative way to engage consumers. With AR, brands can create immersive experiences that allow consumers to interact with products before making a purchase decision.

For example, AR apps that allow consumers to visualize how a piece of furniture will look in their home before buying it, or how a piece of clothing or makeup will look on them. This not only enhances the customer experience but can also increase conversion rates and customer satisfaction.

Blockchain, known for its ability to provide transparency and security, is beginning to be explored in the advertising industry. One of the main challenges in online advertising is the lack of transparency, which can lead to fraud and inefficiencies in advertising spending. Blockchain can help solve this issue by providing an immutable record of transactions, helping ensure that advertisers know exactly where their dollars are being spent. Moreover, Blockchain can facilitate safer and more transparent transactions between parties in the advertising supply chain, such as advertisers, publishers, and consumers.

Beyond these technologies, the integration of advanced analytics and the utilization of big data will continue to be vital for the success of advertising campaigns. Analytical platforms allow advertisers to measure campaign performance in real-time, gain insights on ROI, and optimize strategies to improve engagement and conversions.

The convergence of these emerging technologies is creating a more dynamic and data-driven advertising landscape, where personalization, efficiency, and transparency is paramount. For marketing professionals, staying ahead of these trends and exploring the opportunities they present is crucial to maintaining relevance and effectiveness in an increasingly competitive and technology-driven digital market. Brands that can successfully navigate this evolving landscape will be better positioned to connect with their audiences in a meaningful way and achieve their business objectives in an increasingly digital and interconnected world.

RESEARCH SOURCES

[1] "Data-Driven Strategies for Writing Effective Titles and Headlines." Buffer. 2019.

[2] "How Netflix Uses Data to Drive Marketing Success." Single Grain. 2020.

[3] "10 Companies Using Machine Learning in Cool Ways." WordStream. 2019.

[4] "Data-Driven Marketing: The 15 Metrics Everyone in Marketing Should Know." Neil Patel. 2019.

[5] "The Ultimate Guide to Data-Driven Marketing." SEMrush. 2020.

[6] "How to Create a Data-Driven Marketing Strategy." Sprout Social. 2020.

[7] "The Future of Advertising: What to Expect." Investopedia. 2021.

[8] "How online advertising targets consumers: The uses of categories and ...". Journals Sage Pub.

[9] "What are marketing metrics and why are they important?". Advertising Amazon. 2021.

[10] "Personally relevant online advertisements: Effects of ... - PLOS". Journals Plos Org.

[11] "25 Key Advertising Metrics All Digital Marketers Should Track - Instapage". Instapage.com.

[12] "Complete Guide to Advertising Metrics in 2023: 100+ Benchmark ... - Adriel". Adriel.com.

[13] "How to Measure and Analyze Online Advertising Metrics and KPIs - LinkedIn". LinkedIn.

[14] "Advertising metrics for your bottom-line - Think with Google". Think with Google.

[15] "How Does Social Media Affect Advertising?". Social Media Explorer.

[16] "The Importance of Social Media Advertising". Social Media Today.

[17] "The Future of Digital Advertising: 2021 and Beyond". Business 2 Community.

[18] "AI in Advertising – Current Applications and Future Trends". Emerj.

ABOUT THE AUTHOR

Mauricio Vellasquez is a Brazilian marketing professional with a degree in Business Administration and post-graduate qualifications in Electronics. In his ventures, he has generated seven-figure revenue for digital businesses through Paid Traffic and Search Engine Optimization (SEO). Currently, he is a digital business strategist and conducts research on internet marketing trends and optimizes digital businesses through Data Science and Business Intelligence.